Sheila

Happy Rambling

Michael

18 · 7 · 93

PUBLICATION DETAILS AND CIP DATA ON PAGE 39

MIDSUMMER MORNING JOG LOG

A poem by Michael Horovitz
with drawings by Peter Blake

Five Seasons Press · Hereford · 1986

DEDICATED
in love and homage
to
Frances Horovitz
1938-1983

in this valley she walked
                    I remember
a woman with the smell of wind in her hands
walking at nightfall in the floating dusk
veiled in the petals of an early spring

they say she was made of flowers
flowers yellow and white
                    of spring and summer
and drifted away on wind and water
when the shape spell dissolved

certain she was a flower in our valley . . .

Frances Horovitz

The body dies; the body's beauty lives.
So evenings die, in their green going,
A wave, interminably flowing.

. . . .

Now, in its immortality, it plays
On the clear viol of her memory,
And makes a constant sacrament of praise.

Wallace Stevens

Dances for thee I propose saluting thee, adornments and feastings for thee,
And the sights of the open landscape and the high-spread sky are fitting,
. . . . . . and the huge and thoughtful night
. . . in silence under many a star,
The ocean shore and the husky whispering wave whose voice I know . . . . . .

Over the tree-tops I float thee a song,
Over the rising and sinking waves, over the myriad fields and the prairies wide,
Over the dense-pack'd cities all and the teeming wharves and ways . . .

Walt Whitman

What thou lovest well is thy true heritage
What thou lov'st well shall not be reft from thee

The ant's a centaur in his dragon world.
Pull down thy vanity, it is not man
Made courage, or made order, or made grace,
    Pull down thy vanity, I say pull down.
Learn of the green world what can be thy place
In scaled invention or true artistry . . .

Ezra Pound

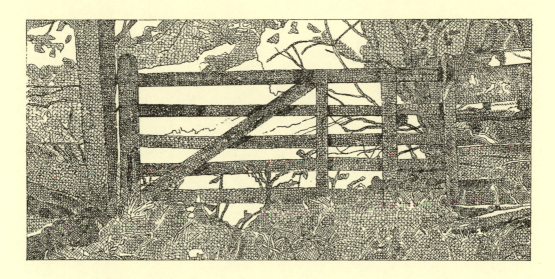

I

    A five barred gate's straight lines assert
the stubborn human will's survival
—absurd, in the mortal coil
of clock-time's inert 'before' and 'after'
such flagrant pink bespattered mornings,
throbbing with lucent light and sound
that wake and drive us
                         from a different metronome:
. . . call of
the wild of flowers, laughter of birds —exempt
from history's grim damper on exuberance
   —at least until
airgun or catapult or cat
                or running man . . .

                                   . . . I glimpse
a handful of the infinite
                  minute particulars
                      I brush across—

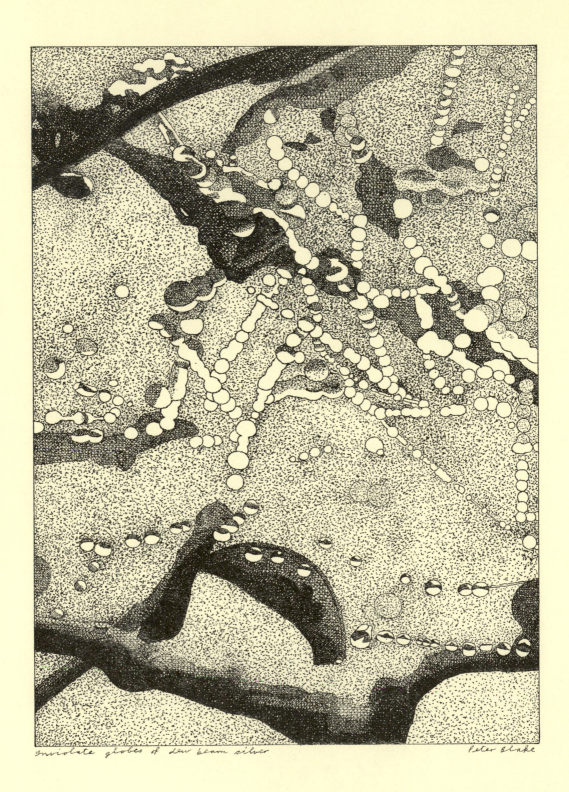

inviolate globes of dew beam silver   Peter Blake

inviolate globes of dew beam silver
                                    satellite reflected planets
    (round each of which—had we but
    an inkling of the microscopic vision—
    might be discerned in turn its myriad
    of star systems, archipelagoes of islets)
    swaying tremulous on brittle, yet bravely
sky-stabbing grassblade tips
                          . . . then whoosh, a spluttering
of deflected sunrays and fernfall and bush in disarray
beclouds my gaze
    —the black and white-feathered close-up flurry
    of a jumbo magpie
    surprised by my cloddy zigzag hops

     —apparition I must seem, leaping blind and deaf
    to the fleet-winged early warning
notes of my advent
                relayed from the lanesides
                              all over the valley
    —so brutishly revelling
    in my refracted halo, vicarious godhead
    of being

     —The First up
                and out—ha!
    jigging and bopping
    with ludicrously heavy-booted feet
        to avoid the upsurge here
        of a sun-spatted puddle,

there the liquidation
of an innocent slug or snail
   (though I've heard tell some regard
   these mild slithing creatures
   as enemies of growth
— good growth of fodder for the worstest beast, they mean)

   . . . I'd never seen a beige-brown slug before — like acorns
in the delicacy of its compactly fitting two-toned sheen
and seemingly precision built
as the other sort of slug that's shot from guns

      — or was it after all a snail I just missed
      killing on the path
somehow severed from its shell? Too late
      to find out now, till the next
      — and gentler — foray of field work
      into the creepy-crawly universe

      — than which a lot worse
      I could do, oft have

. . . but here see how
small *is* beautiful

         (. . galaxies unbehent
         in the realms of office and gold dug or spent
         from plush seats in the sanitised upper grand

self-satisfied circle swelling its gland
with caviar, champagne, game pie and the grind
of dry wit and dry bones on dry land
with no tremor of thought or hint of a rind
for the burrowing souls bearing fardels behind
the nether skirting of the wine cellar and beyond
the bijou patio's outer frond —
the molehill, the dung-beetle, horsefly and
the populous progeny, wriggling quietly, unplanned
of earwig, industrious ant and worm
that squirm and scuttle and writhe beneath you
all unconsidered . . . . .

                                             till one by chance,
or emboldened by curiosity or hunger, aspire
to your æthereal level — bathroom floor, or yet higher
intrude to the hem of your untouchable standing
or sitting — or lying, even . . .

                                        . . to be noticed at last
— and instantly, ruthlessly, zapped to the past
with fearful shrieks, disinfectants and aspersions cast
including the contemptuous designation: *bug*
which gets applied indiscriminately to flea, snail and slug)

   . . . for all that
it may be proved such beings do
defile the farmer's furrowed orders
or variously (as a spin-off) bug the citizens,
it feels wrong to me that we
should therefore make so free

to grind our shamelessly cowhidebound heels
full in their barely believable faces,
flattening their last stays and traces
like the would-be genocidal wipeout
of rabbits, badgers, partridge, whales

. . . should we not rather pity,
therefore *dis*endanger them
no less than herons, otters, singing seals,

for *every thing that lives is Holy*

though — heaven help us —
if every anthill and cobweb
be thus close considered,
the murder of getting on for
maybe many million flies
and all manner of other tiny insects
crowds daily, nightly, thicker on our hands
(and remember:
each little mite
we're inclined to hate
is life size and 4D —all
the world to its mate)
and by that same strict token, niceties for lice
and mice — what about king rats?

And should I not then keep my cat
forever chained upon the mat?

. . . . Not very nice for her; but
the local birds and voles and shrews
would certainly breathe easier and
in their several manors, newly unmolested, raise
the kind of multilateral cheer of a lifetime
pacifists and eco-nuts might vent
if governments of the world could really get together
and ban the bomb — all bombs

II

. . . the mind is swiftly boggled by such sums
the ramifications recede, dissolve as
on I charge and stumble
squishing now and then against remains
of the countless deaths whose predatory nature
night's blanket harboured, each and all
unbeknown to me (as was — safe and soundproofed
and plastered indoors):

— then something moving in my hair
arrests me in my tracks   . . . limp-
wristedly I pick it out
and as gingerly fling it from me —

                                        . . . only a spider
        whose undeterred and neatly patterned
        walk-off up an elder
        rebukes my broody speculations
            — its purposive calligraphy
            puts my sprawling scrawl to shame

making me feel way out of touch,
a freakishly blundering four-eyed goon
— still dafter in my stoned-out scribbling
about the mystical bodies and souls of flies
when my unruly locks were webbed
(are wreathèd still) with a detritus
of spider-cordoned corses

    — all heedless of
any life other
than the image that comes up next . . . as of any
    bird or buglet being so mental
as to waste trees by encouraging reading or writing
— let alone the idea of dolphins say, or frogs
directing cameras underwater
        so . .
                . . must get me out
                                    from under

these knots I can't untie
so far from the sainted smithy of the soul;   yet

what else to do but accept myself
and draw deep breaths
savouring as best I may
a gust of all the smells
that blow my way

— panting, alternately exultant and aghast, ope' mouthed
to be suddenly all but gassed by fumes so chock
and palpable — crushed carnationlike density
of lush night-scented stocks, soft
clotting by remote control the air
of this already brimful blaze of daybreak

. . . awhirl with honking pheasant, community panic
at my every seven-league signalled step
— near electrified whirr of wings
abuzz in outrage, but powerless
before this tankine tremor that scatters
nests, settlements, plantations — plangent parliaments
of fowl . . . . :   blue, browny-pink and grey of jay,
flash of doves alarmed, and chittering chorister wrens
and clerical caw-cawing crows in a flap
huffily removing
                              to loftier branches
                                                  in farther fields
of a less (*caw-caw*) vulgarised class of diocese

The innermost nave of the abbey of trees   Peter Blake

. . . yet from
        the innermost nave
    of the abbey of trees
   I pass under hardly half aware
  my piston-headed routine jogging desecrates
   an aural filigree of matinal orisons —
though the confidential cooing
of wood pigeons
grows plaintive
    . . . still the steady
(albeit ever
so slightly distant)
   chiffchaff of the chiffchaff
chiffchaffs on,
unfazed heartbeat of syncopation

amid the manifold upraised and burbling beaks
conjoined in symphonic clamour
welcoming new day

  now springs the spray
  and sprays the spring

        —and yet, giving voice to some dismay

        now also cumbers the lurch
        twixt bracken and birch
        of this too well sullied flesh

             . . . still relishing
delight of mist milled shafts
of luminous high holy lights —
of rising sun piercing holes through trees
— dappling paths to heaven, and leaves to earth
and piebald breeze-stirred leafshadows
to birth
              — though : is it not
                          the foliage
                          first moving
                          casts the shadows
                          into movement
              — can shadows
              'in themselves' be said
              to move
                          at all ?
                          All
              I can say is, today
                                      a small commotion
                          of nascent shadows
                                      caught my eye

— their dance

intermingling with my own

and with the play of sunlight

on the pathway

suggesting Wordsworthian other presences —
the presence of Wordsworth's vision itself — watching
with those of Shelley, Milton, Chaucer —
immortal the lineaments of every plant
and shrub and flower Blake saw
and transcribed an earlier morn:

" . . . . . first the Wild Thyme
And Meadow-sweet, downy & soft waving among the reeds,
Light springing on the air, lead the sweet Dance: they wake
The Honeysuckle sleeping on the Oak; the flaunting beauty
Revels along upon the wind; the White-thorn, lovely May,
Opens her many lovely eyes listening; the Rose still sleeps,
None dare to wake her; soon she bursts her crimson curtain'd bed
And comes forth in the majesty of beauty; every Flower,
The Pink, the Jessamine, the Wall-flower, the Carnation,
The Jonquil, the mild Lilly, opes her heavens; every Tree
And Flower & Herb soon fill the air with an innumerable Dance,
Yet all in order sweet & lovely.   Men are sick with Love . . ."

III

—of weeds, even . . . . almost
                              —in my jungle of a garden—
                              especially the weeds:

                    give them an inch of poetic licence,
                        they'll run riot for barnyards and more
                    making hay of the seedpacket pennanted rows
                        of kemptitudes of yore

                    pent-up wild and woody pentameters
                        well out and take root by the score
                    till inside we're all sleeping beauties
                        unable to hear ourselves snore
                    —never mind the postman prince crashing
                        and bashing, baffled at the door

. . . . . barred by battalions,
barricades of weeds revolutionary—
weeds upon weeds in abundancy swirling
and thrusting their spears in brazen pride
blocking the glades,
                              ever shifting shades
of shimmering starspun wood anemone teenies,
then groves of garlic, twinkling like sparklers
or revolving light-orbs in a darkened palais
—fairy fays on parade, breathtakingly perfumed
and retaining their cools, in the hot face and frenzy
of bramble-tailed satyrs and jumping jack hogweeds

—jostling, and hoicking up their joint-ends
every which way, agog
to hog the whole show
        but policed by serrated nettle's tall columns,
        giant rhubarb and blood-veined dock leaves,
    with heraldic vetch grouped like *corps de ballet*
    holding their sugarplum pose, though encircled
by dazed bumblebees, parched at summer's high noon
—thirsty for opening-time—roaming and swarming
        from the glinting russet barb-wiry strands
        —dervish-whorled nether thickets
        of my foxy dame sorrel,
leading up to a tangle of unmade beds
brimming with rough thorn-cloth'd rosebudded limbs—
    all hips and haws and pips and paws
    leaning and heaving, flexing their claws
        like some fungoid group grope
        drugged to 'go with the flow'
        in berserk rugger scrums
        from hedgerow to compost

        . . . lusty clustering teams of weeds
    closing ranks with stray blooms
    and campion followers and farther off-breeds
    to touch down and strike home, and kick off anew
        though the goal posts from each other
        are long lost to view

    —overrun by the champions:
    Cow Parsley 69   Ragged Robins 2

. . . . *Dog Rose Ramblers v. Lords-and-Ladies*
abandoned in dread of the showers
of aggro supporting the Ladies'
equal right to sportive Misrule
        —to have done with nursing their flowers
    and shaping up to the tool

    . . . . for the Ladies

                        bored with being subjected
    to the rapt rolling out of the mast
        —with unfurling their monk's cowl vulvas
    so verdant, moist and vast
    would have done with holy orders and get
    their sap-laden rocks off at last:

                            —*Oh,*
    To have done with the long-drawn-out waiting
    To get our cherries red and hard
            On naked peduncles aquiver
            And explode the sticky seed
                            . . . *Yes,*
    How we long for lovebirds to get mating —
    Get your beaks stuck in and give head
            —Open our gates of paradise,
            Let heaven's glory be spread
                            . . . *Aah,*
    Come   —chew on these bunches of berries
    And help get the good news spread —

22

. . . from cock-crowing shoots in the seedbed
and blue-blooded asparagus tips
pushing up mottled and juicy, hard
by the poppies' flaring wide lips

— from the toe of coltsfoot's thick rootstock
up its soft furry-scaled spiral stairs
to the hoary round fruit-swollen wombhead
— getting spring fever's prayers widespread

. . . from dandelion kisses blown blithely
to midsummer madness, run wild
— tearing loose and fast as a calendar's pages
when yearning sadness turns to gladness
— though it fly against the grain
                              of the politically desirable
                              state of the nation, spreading careless
                              orgiastic proliferation
voracious for pleasure, careless of pain
re-enacting the fall all over again

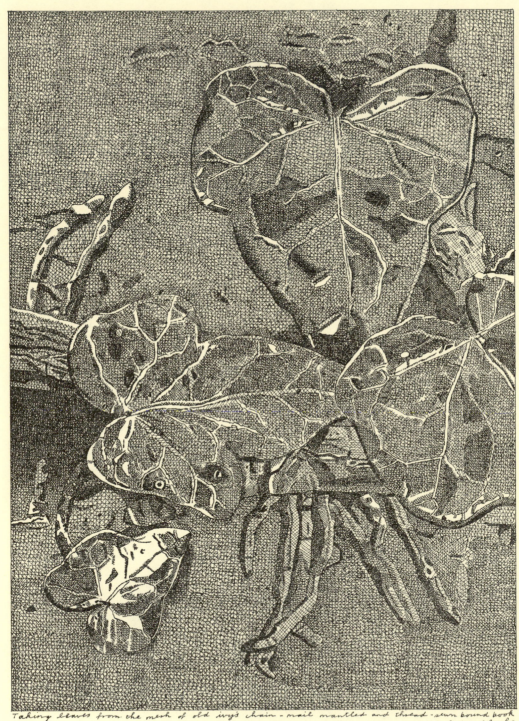

Taking leaves from the mesh of old ivy's chain-mail mantled and thread-sewn bound book

Peter Blake

—taking leaves from the mesh of old ivy's
chain-mail mantled and thread-sewn bound book,
    creeping bindweed rears up and lunges
    and clasps, stealing more than a look
       'neath Queen Anne's lace traceries
       —twirling pink-faced embraceries
    up her ladies' smocks all in a row
       . . . serpentining the ground,
         there   —it winds itself round
          —and in,
            and out,
               and tight about
      every floral skirt it can find

. . . . . and like old man's beard,
           hairy cleavers
scramble and goose at each bush—
tickling the spines of young fruit trees
and cleaving live meat in their rush
      for th' indelible purplish imprint
      trailed by their prickly-glue kiss
      clings to fur and feather, any weather

      —storm waters can't quench
             the fire of their love
      —its insatiable flame but increaseth:
its hugs would fain strangle the shires of the Angle
overcoming those spruce clumps of mint
   —enwrap all the flowers of the isles with its wiles,
ruthless squeezing and biting and pinching and rutting
bruised herbs till their juice is quite spent

—bending even the Englishest rose to its bidding,
set to ravish each one stemless
                              for fun

IV

                                        . . . *O Rose*
                                        —lost fragrance

        lemon mint
        —whose tang

                        —but away, nostalgia
                        —Veil'd Melancholy, hence
            fly with osprey or plover,
            or delight in the temple
            thrown up by the bristling
            silver thistle
                        over clover—
            shining buttercup
        and cowslip
        going down on
                        and under
        many a blushful
        lass and her lover
            turning the good earth
            over and over
                and one another
                the whole world over

—turning each other
over and over
—girl into mother,
lover to brother
to husband the garden
turning the whole
rich earth over
and over

and while bees idly wonder
whether to bother
to sip cuckoo pints foamy
with frog-hopper squirts,
cuckoos call from the forest
come out of the closet

and herb robert winks
at families of mushrooms,
toy henges or cloisters
huddled round streams
where deep green and yellowing
watercress glitters
tinged with the stale
visitations of horses

at grass with their foals

—on sudden fresh-frisking
trampling and tumbling
spontaneous combustion
—and as quickly stock-still
and earnest again

exhaling thin smoke
nuzzling willowherb
and mosses, silent hooved
crunching greenery
nameless to me

                                    . . . . as

yonder pale sky
-blue high butterfly
going the rounds
of an inexhaustible harem
of wild thymes immemorial
with a long tongue for nectar
— but can it distinguish
puce from lilac
or the greater
                from a lesser
celandine?

           . . . Ah — holla there — silent
Sunflower!
                Forget-me-not —

                                    your smiles
                light up
                      the soul of the world
        my soul belongs to, now

I forget not you

and begin
to look — and perceive
the one unbounded
primeval garden — its seeds
and springs
                    like first light
never lost

   since the very first dawn

— to listen, and hear
again,
                    distantly
gathering trills
of the unending concert
of spiritual sensation
in which I apprehend

   all our steps are envelopt

   . . . . like the petalfaced
   grenades of pollen — like nectaries
   poised to exude
   honeydew, ambrosia . . . of
"that sweet golden clime"
                    that gleams
in Samuel Palmer's vaulted sheepscapes
raining amber light from Cotswold stone
through happy fields, here and now

—celestial in the sense of wordless
but grounded

       —like these gaggles
    of new lambs exploring
     their enormous orchard,
straining wobbly legs for precedence
at the fleecy private bar;

     like these blotchy bevies
    of bullocks that snort
at tough tussocks and sheepdogs
and joggers and wasps

—grounded in light, like John Clare's Calendar
     —light springing loamy
    from fresh-watered tilth
    imbuing the air
    with ripe succulent balm

                . . . . springs

           of wisdom

. . . . seeds

of joy —

V

Earth's energy
like fish   from fish
—or iris
dilating
to iris . . .
—like pollen   keeps darting
– out   and on   & round
twirling   sycamore keys   to unlock
—transform . . .   . . . outface—
the more and more
closely   binding
inexorable
mobile   mosaic
of intertwined
death–in–life . . . . life–in–death
—shedding leaves   spilling seeds—

composting

—hiving—

– declining –

yet still

. . reviving . .

piecing itself

. . . . together withal . . . .

. . . with all its crawling and fluttering denizens
tunnelling and buzzing, sawing
and subtly trumpeting on
in muted solos or dizzy glissandi
or descanting, or glistering within
the lights and darks of other wafting
winds and reeds and woods —
dead elm and evergreen, broken
bluebell, trampoline
of runner bean and columbine
arcing and curling
where the brook purls
through a clearing;
heather bell and harebell
mount with bugles — pell-mell
flickering and flaring
and jamming blues with buskers
and small groups, burgeoning —
soon to grow to big bands — orchestras
with massed bluebells standing
hunched or cupping upward
in unison with Pan
and God and Mother Nature,
hymning high summer's heyday
of cockerel paging pimpernel
and asphodel
and Morrismen,
with ne'er-do-well and infidel
made completely good again
by falling down a wishing well

   —maids and farmhands come away

to chase and play
the rites of Flora's holiday,
   her children romp intrepidly
  on dry-stone walls, right merrily
     and all the while the roundelays
     of songbirds pump the revelry
     o'er spinneys, dells
       and gardens embroidered
       in herbaceous jamboree
       with soapwort and stitchwort,
        lady's bedstraw, sneezewort—
        musk mallow, milkwort,
        nipplewort and navelwort

—vexed gardeners, though, chase litterbugs
across bones and plastic glasswort,
and as they slither on the dregs
of bottle savaged ragwort
they mutter darkly how they wish
such spirits never blithe wert . . .

       yet worms writhe on—and thrive from
       nonstop bibbing of clean earth dirt
      —spent bladderwort just one more twist
      to their pattern of all patients

   —yes; the cut worm forgives the plough
  as firewood the chain saw
in the pattern ever changing, constant
using
   —used by—
       everything that lives

. . . . matching, cross-hatching
intro- and extrovert
pervert with convert —
Ginsberg to George Herbert,

Coleridge spooning dropwort
whilst Dorothy and William
take his hemp nettle sherbert
with a sharp pinch of saltwort

and their inward eyes flash outward
questing local habitations
for the airy shapes and rills
that haunt our ancient lakes and hills

. . . hatching shapes half seen
on shapes unseen
and massy groundworks
and secret invisible
funnels and forces (invisible
to passing scalèd eyes)

— force of animal wonderment
Whitman embodied — unbuttoned, as it came
— "Calling
. . . from flower-beds, vines, tangled underbrush . . . .
Far-swooping elbow'd earth — rich apple-blossom'd earth"
— united states of feeling, of
being —
ever open —
"Laved in the flood of thy bliss" —

Alleluia!

      . . . . . . Vistas that beckoned
hassock-bent Hopkins's rhythms to spring
and fern-fledged Dylan Thomas to sing
in praise of green fuses seen plain at the heart
of the skipping hill psalms of David and Smart
and Keats's deep forest of faery art—
of the madrigal, maypole, fauns' feast and spread wing
from where Spenser's woods did answer

                        —do today
their Eccho ring

              . . . to the song stilled skies
of Edward Thomas too, who liked
    "As well as any bloom upon a flower
    . . . . the dust on the nettles, never lost
    Except to prove the sweetness of a shower"

      . . . . . . sweet fruits
these spoils of my harvester toils
in the bower of midnight oils
feed love's dreams
            to awaken and mark
       like Shakespeare's Ant, agape
with renewed first truth—
as that
                "Here is my space,
      Kingdoms are clay: our dungy earth alike
      Feeds beast as man"

. . . . . hence inspirited afresh
with earth's unstoppable hurrah

   to leap with birds in mid Heaven
     —know all's
(more or less—) well with the worm,

share with fellow ramblers and passengers
the ownerless good cheer
                        and echo, too, the silence
of these voices, these visions
—these heavenly hosts
          of ox-eye daisies
        sprinkling white and yellowgold
      the railway banks
     our grimy windows cut through
   on good days—as if
   to prove . . . . how much more neatly
vegetation
     arranges and disports itself
than clumsy humankind

yet all this perfect order and profusion
is bestowed on us

to ravage   —or relish,
           nurture
              and replenish,

                     Yea!

And to marvel at earths heavenly hosts of ox-eye daisies

Peter Blake

Author's Note

Special thanks are due

✗ to Frances Horovitz, Inge Laird, Kathleen Raine, Chris Torrance and Heathcote Williams who — in their several inimitable ways — helped me toward the completion of this verse with corrections and advice on textual and botanical details;

✗ to Glenn Storhaug for his belief in the work and implementation thereof with this inspired master-printing and design;

✗ and to Peter Blake for his perfect illustrations on pages 7, 8, 16, 24 and 37.

The piece was composed at intervals between June 1981 and September '85 in The Scrubs — a remote wooded offshoot of the Slad Valley, Gloucestershire. It underwent many changes, with several versions considerably longer than this one; whose last page was further revised in response to Peter's unblinking 'day's eye' daisies. Although he's never been here, each of these drawings is alive with the essential feelings, atmosphere and minutiæ which first set the lines they interpret into motion.

M H, 16 September 1985

Acknowledgements

The photographs on the cover are by Allan Burgis (Michael Horovitz on left) and Joan Williams (Peter Blake on right).

The eleven lines from *An Old Man Remembers* by Frances Horovitz are reprinted from her *Collected Poems* (1985) by kind permission of her editor and literary executor Roger Garfitt and the joint publishers Bloodaxe Books and Enitharmon Press. The two stanzas from the close of Wallace Stevens's *Peter Quince at the Clavier* on page 5 (from *The Collected Poems* of Wallace Stevens) and the Ezra Pound epigraph on page 6 (from Canto LXXXI of the *Pisan Cantos of Ezra Pound*) are reprinted by kind permission of Faber & Faber Ltd. The lines by Walt Whitman on page 5 are from section 14 of *When Lilacs Last in the Dooryard Bloom'd*. The lines quoted on page 19 are from William Blake's *Milton* (Book the Second, 34); the phrase quoted on page 29 is from Blake's *Ah! Sun-flower*; the quotations on page 34 are from Walt Whitman's *Song of Myself* and *When Lilacs Last in the Dooryard Bloom'd*; and the quotations on page 35 are from *Tall Nettles* by Edward Thomas, and Shakespeare's *Antony and Cleopatra* (I.i. 34-36).

This first trade edition (in both cloth and paper bindings) is printed letterpress on 100 %
recycled paper from hand set 14pt Ehrhardt type first used for the special boxed edition
(100 copies printed on hand made paper in 1985). This edition printed and published
in the early spring of 1986 at Five Seasons Press, Madley, Hereford HR2 9NZ, England.

British Library Cataloguing in Publication Data

Horovitz, Michael
    Midsummer morning jog log.
    1. Title
    821'.914   PR6058.0714

ISBN 0-9504606-7-2
ISBN 0-9504606-8-0 Pbk